FAVORITE CLASSICS

arranged for brass quintet
by Henry Charles Smith

intermediate   level

THE CANADIAN BRASS

CANADIAN
BRASS
SERIES OF
COLLECTED QUINTETS

GAVOTTE
from the *6th Cello Suite*

J. S. Bach
(1685-1750)
arranged by Henry Charles Smith

HORN

PRAYER
from *Hansel and Gretel*

Engelbert Humperdinck
(1854 - 1921)
arranged by Henry Charles Smith

HORN

CANTATE DOMINO

HORN

Giuseppe Ottavio Pitoni
(1657-1743)
arranged by Henry Charles Smith

*Play the piece twice through; no ritard. nor fermata the first time.

THE LIBERTY BELL

HORN

John Philip Sousa
(1854 - 1932)
arranged by Henry Charles Smith

QUESTO E QUELLA

from *Rigoletto*

HORN

Giuseppe Verdi
(1813 - 1901)
arranged by Henry Charles Smith

PILGRIM'S CHORUS

from *Tannhauser*

HORN

Richard Wagner
(1813 - 1883)
arranged by Henry Charles Smith

CANADIAN BRASS
SERIES OF COLLECTED QUINTETS

FAVORITE CLASSICS

arranged for brass quintet
by Henry Charles Smith

contents

Welcome to the *Canadian Brass Series of Collected Quintets.* In our work with students, for some time we have been aware of the need for more brass quintet music at easy and intermediate levels of difficulty. We are continually observing a kind of "Renaissance" in brass music, not only in audience responses to our quintet, but to all brass music in general. The brass quintet, as a chamber ensemble, seems to have become as standard a chamber combination as a string quartet. That could not have been said twenty-five years ago. Brass quintets are popping up everywhere — professional quintets, junior and senior high school ensembles, college and university groups, and amateur quintets of adult players.

We have carefully chosen the literature for these collected quintets, and closely supervised the arrangements. Our aim was to retain a Canadian Brass flavor to each arrangement, and create attractive repertory designed so that any brass quintet can play it with satisfying results. We've often remarked to one another that we certainly wish that we'd had quintet arrangements like these when we were students!

— THE CANADIAN BRASS

U.S. $7.99
ISBN-13: 978-1-4584-0174-8
Distributed By

50488786   9 781458 401748

HAL•LEONARD®